SEO Organics

Easy Search Engine Optimization

By B.A. Pogreba

My search engine optimization tips will increase website traffic and Internet ranking via simple content changes, free links and video marketing.

No computer or web design degree needed!

Save hundreds to thousands of dollars and follow these simple steps or have a web designer do it.

****

Google AdWords and Pay per Click are not necessary to get high placement on the Internet.

Keywords are mostly out. Link Exchanges can cause your website to be de-ranked by Google. Organic Search Engine Optimization is where it's at.

Get your website ranked high on Google NOW.

SIMPLE STEPS for SUCCESS

1. *Know Your Business*

2. *Designing the Home Page including Header Box, Main Box and Bottom Box frames.*

3. *Keywords and Meta Description / Title*

4. *Updating content and photos*

5. *YouTube – a great source of free advertising*

6. *Submit to Search Engines, local directories*

7. *Google Account*

8. *Google Images and Picasa web*

9. *Quality Links*

10. *Visit your own site often.*

Copyright 2012 by B. A. Pogreba

1. KNOW YOUR BUSINESS

Write Down words and phrases as key info to refer to that describe your business including area cities regardless if you have a storefront or if customers go to your location.

On your home page, put in order the <u>most important words first</u> that both describe your business or service and include the cities in the surrounding area if it's relevant to what you do.

Write a phrase or sentence that makes sense out of those words without any commas or punctuation. That phrase should be brief and added to the top and/or bottom of your title with variation if both.

Repeats of key info are necessary for search engines to find your site as templates are usually read separately by search engines and further increase your placement on the web.

Be sure to put that key info at or near the beginning of the paragraph each time without commas or punctuations including dashes.

2. DESIGNING THE HOME PAGE

Many websites have frames of different boxes. Each one is important in placing similar words and phrases that describe your business.

Search engines primarily grab words on the header (top box) of the home page, main center box and the very bottom of the page.

Write similar but not identical words and phrases at the beginning of those frames. It will seem like repeats and website designers usually avoid it but it is necessary if you want visibility and high ranking.

If your website is mostly one blank page, the first words are still key to grabbing searches and the remaining content will not be as important as websites with different frames or boxes which can be read separately by search engines.

Follow the examples below for further specifics on Headings, Main or Center box and bottom area of the website home page.

EXAMPLE of Existing Website Heading:

Event Planning by MaryLou
909-909-0000 marylou@eventplanning.com
We are experts at party planning!

CHANGE TO:

Party and Meeting Planners in Phoenix welcomes
***Event Planning by MaryLou** for weddings and*
corporate parties with full service and catering.
909-909-0000 - marylou@eventplanning.com

The name of this business: "***Event Planning by** ...*"
is a good generic search term but won't capture the
area it serves – such as Phoenix – and some will
search "party" or "parties" rather than "event" and
some will search "Planners" rather than "Planning."

The new heading in small font helps capture search
engines and also makes sense as a sentence. It's
meant for SEO more than readers. Now this title will
capture searches for party, meeting, planners,
Phoenix, event, planning, MaryLou, weddings,
corporate, parties, full service, catering.

Note: No commas or punctuation.

This will capture searches within a few days to a few weeks – depending on the rotation and update cycle by Google.

If your business specializes in a particular type of party planning like bar mitzvahs, those words can replace "corporate parties" or "weddings" etc.

The top line in smaller font size still makes sense by itself but does not stand out. Font size does not matter for searches but making it too small (8 pt) or changing the font color to blend in with the background or be invisible (looks less cluttered but still grab search engines) is called "Black Hat SEO" and Google will **de-rank** your website if it is discovered. DO NOT DO IT.

Keep it short, simple and don't bother to try and grab every possible search word at the top. There are other ways to capture searches besides a website. All of the ones I know of are included in this book.

Website designers are often visual and avoid word clutter or repeating information. But this rules needs to be broken or the traffic could remain low for your website.

Your company name can also have added words or phrases following the title, above or under the title. However, DO NOT jam too many words or make it look like keywords. **IT MUST MAKE SENSE** as a brief sentence in order to avoid de-ranking of your website by Google and other sites that follow.

EXAMPLE of Existing Website Title (or bottom of page as well):

Joe's Plumbing Company
123 Main St. Akron, OHIO
123-555-1234

CHANGE TO

Joe's Plumbing Company of Akron
offers affordable plumber services including
sewer cleanouts and small repairs.
123-555-1234
(add address at end if you have a storefront)

Now the title will grab searches for affordable, plumbing **and** plumber, Akron, sewer, cleanouts and repairs. Akron can be written "Akron OH" or "Akron area."

A company address is only needed on the front page if it's a storefront but never written in the details on the top of the page as it just delays the word "Akron" being found or other words more important than 123 Main St. If you include your address, avoid 123 Main St. Akron, Ohio or
123 Main St, Akron, OH

Instead: **123 Main St Akron OH + Zip Code**
Note: no commas or periods.

Zip Codes help capture localized searches if customer puts in a zip code or their IP address is a close match.

Commas and other punctuation break up search engine results.

Know you cannot fit every word or key phrase on your page but there are other ways to accomplish this in video marketing and free directories.

This also applies to any place online you put your business address. Avoid commas and punctuation.

These rules also apply for main and bottom boxes.

MAIN BOX FRAME EXAMPLES:

EXAMPLE of current website main / center box (generally has the most content on webpage):

"We have been in business for 19 years and customer service is our first priority. Call us for a free estimate! We stand by our quotes!"

CHANGE TO:

"Our catering company in Phoenix has enjoyed planning weddings and corporate parties for 20 years and we welcome inquiries for free estimates."

Note that the first example will not capture search engines because it doesn't say what this business does or the city or area it serves.

Although the header is the main attraction for search engines, repeating the words in the main box and bottom box will help add even more results.

Google also looks for content that describes a business in detail (like geographic areas) as they view it as more valuable content.

BOTTOM BOX

This is generally a small box and if in a pre-designed template, asks for the name of business, address and zip, etc.

This box can be used as a further description of your business.

EXAMPLE of Current Bottom Box:

"Joe's Plumbing Company, 123 Main St, Akron, OH 012345 800-800-8000"
<u>CHANGE TO:</u>

"Akron Plumbing Services, Joe's Plumbing at 123 Main St, Akron, OH….."

Or
"Joe's Affordable Plumbing Services in Akron, 123 Main St, Akron…"

The lines for name, address, etc., are often broken up and the first line is the most important but as always, don't clutter with too many words and remember it must look like a brief sentence.

A business that goes to the customer locations makes the address of that business less important. If a business serves Denver but is based in nearby Brighton, the city of Brighton need not be mentioned at all or at the tail end of a page if most of the customer calls are based in Denver.

EXAMPLE of Current Bottom Box:

(commas represent separate lines that might be in place to fill in but if there are no separate lines, just write them with no commas that still makes sense):

"Joe's Plumbing Company, 123 Elm, Brighton CO, 800-800-8000"

CHANGE TO:

"Denver area plumbing services, Joe's Plumbing Company, Affordable and Same Day service Brighton, CO, 800-800-8000."

Keywords and Meta Description are still important for other search engines just not for Google.

However, it's still worth taking the time to ensure they're accurate and at their best capability.

3. KEYWORDS and META DESCRIPTION TITLE:

EXAMPLE of Current Keywords:

Joe's Plumbing Company, plumbing services, plumbing needs, plumbing repairs, plumbing companies, plumbing company,

Nothing in these keywords captures the location so it might be buried along with any plumbing company in the country or world.

Most will be looking for a plumbing company they don't know the name of so no need to put it in the keywords as it just delays them finding the more important words that follow (plumbing services, etc.). A website named "Joe's Plumbing Company" will be found in a search without those keywords since those words are on found the content on the website page.
CHANGE TO:

Plumbing, services, Akron, plumbers, affordable, repairs, companies, (nearby town), (another nearby town), Joe's, Joe, ...

There's no need to repeat "plumbing" in a search term as the individual words "plumbing" and "services" will capture a lot of searches.

Also try to write keywords in an order that folks might type in a search term phrase such as "Plumbing repairs Akron" but as individual keywords such as: plumbing, services, Akron, etc.

You can add "Joe's" or "Joe" to the keywords to capture those who don't know the full or correct name of the company and might say "Joe the plumber" in a search. But leave these keywords further down the list.

Many search engines don't read past 250 characters for keywords, so approximately 25 - 30 keywords is a good range and start with the most important words first.

Meta Description and Title in source page:

EXAMPLE of CURRENT Title or Description:

"Events Planning by MaryLou" or

"Special Event planners"

CHANGE TO:

*"Event Planning by Phoenix party planner
MaryLou"*

This once again captures event, planning, Phoenix,
party and planner as well as MaryLou."

I do not suggest straying far from the official name
to avoid any de-ranking by Google – just a better
description that also captures search results.

4. UPDATING CONTENT & PHOTOS
*Update photos and a few words at least a couple of
times a year* (more if possible) to keep content fresh.
This includes the phrase lines – even if just
switching them back and forth with one subtle
change of a word or two. Google sees this as a more
valuable website with new information.

My guess is they give more weight to websites with new or updated information so their search engine has the latest and best information on the web.

EXAMPLE of Current content on webpage:

"Affordable plumber services in Akron area including sewer cleanouts and small repairs."

UPDATE TO (on occasion):

"Plumbing services in Akron OH area including small repairs and sewer cleanouts."

Then go back to the original one a few months later.

5. YOU TUBE

YouTube is a great marketing tool as customers want to see photos and video for more information. And because it's free, it's a no brainer to use it. Many underestimate or don't recognize its value.

Videos can include –
- A general overview of your product or service
- Multiple videos of specific values of your business

- Testimonials from customers
- Free Tips on your industry

Once on YouTube, other sites (if embedding is allowed – which you should allow) will pick up the videos giving you more exposure.

ALWAYS add or say your website, ph. # or both on the video itself. It can be a continuous video stream or added content at beginning or end of video or both.

If you only include your contact info on the YouTube content box below the video, you risk others linking, embedding or using that video without leading customers to your business – which is the reason for doing videos in the first place.

Saying your company at least twice in the video is also important but avoid making it seem like a commercial or customers might not continue watching it. It needs to be useful, entertaining or both.

Put yourself in their place – What would you want to know about a particular product or service and why would they want your company?

Do you offer better prices?
Faster service?
Same day service?
Open weekends?
Serve a larger area?
Have a higher quality product?
Do you offer more variety others do not?
Do you guarantee your product or service?

To use YouTube for search results, write the most effective keyword type sentence that makes sense:

Title of Video needs to have keywords that don't look like keywords and include location if that is important to your business.

Each video should have different words in the title but can have many of the same ones. Your goal is to capture different search results.

EXAMPLE for Joe's Plumbing Company Title:

1. Plumbing Services Akron area repair tips for toilets

2. How to repair a sink leak tip by Akron OH plumber

3. Joe's Plumbing Company Akron Oh affordable plumber services

You can usually squeeze a few more words in but don't overdo it as my guess is Google might weed out YouTube keyword jammers soon since they purchased YouTube.

TAGS:
I have found individual words work better than groups of words but you can try either or both ways if you have 2 or more videos.

EXAMPLE:
Plumber, plumbing, services, Akron, repair, affordable, sewer, cleanouts, toilet, same day, Joe's, company, business - and / or – Akron plumbing business, plumbing services Akron OH, etc.
Also add other cities you serve high on the tag lines.

If location is important to your business, always add it to the title and tags and put them early in the tags. I suggest no more than 15 tag words or phrases.

DESCRIPTION BOX:

Include your ph # and website and those should be first. Any other details (such as same day service, etc) is secondary so your contact info stands out.

All of the above is on the "Basic Info" page which is the default page for YouTube video info.

Next go to **"Advanced Settings"** – many miss this. It includes geographic location and date of video that is likely essential to Google updates. It also includes options to allow comments on your video.

I suggest not allowing comments to avoid rude people and profane words. Some are just trolls while others can be competitors.

I uncheck the box - or - check it for "Approved" meaning the comment will be emailed to you for approval to post on the page. If it's a nice comment, you can approve it for all to see.

I choose to uncheck all the rest of the boxes. Ratings and thumbs up and down are not of value to you because there is nothing official about the ranking.

CAPTION CERTIFICATION:

Choose "This video has never aired in the U.S." My theory is this helps place your video in higher ranking as it's seen as fresh or unique content.

ALLOW EMBEDDING – Yes.

This will allow other sites to link it and just adds to your exposure in general.

Notify Subscribers – optional

VIDEO LOCATION:

This is essential if you have a storefront or local service but I suggest doing it even if you don't. It appears to help ranking even for those that don't need a geographic location for reasons I haven't yet figured out. Perhaps IP Addresses figure into this.

RECORDING DATE:

This is essential and I sometimes renew dates on

some videos because they might effect ranking. Of course you always make a new video, too.

VIDEO STATISTICS:
I usually uncheck this box as I have a theory it might one day effect video search results but I have it check marked on some of my videos so I cover both sides just in case.

I have seen YouTube videos appear on Google searches an hour after going live.
Perhaps Google now owning YouTube helps.

Go through your videos periodically and note the ones that are getting more views than others. Study if the title, tag lines, date of video or other factors might be the reason. Change the lower viewed videos with a new word in the title or new tag words, etc.

6. <u>SUBMIT TO SEARCH ENGINES AND LOCAL DIRECTORIES</u>

Submit your site to Bing, Yahoo, Jade and more. Search "Free Website Submissions." SubmitExpress.com is one I recommend.

Search free directories for your town or state and join them with an email address you don't mind getting spam or junk mail because it's likely.

Search city, county and state sites to join and a national website that serves major cities – ie: Denver.com, SanFranciso.com, etc. and you submit your site free. Search "Free Directories (my city)"

Many free directories goal is that you will upgrade and pay a monthly fee and by not doing so, you risk someone else able to change the info on your site or simply add their own title if they're a competitor but the risk of this is relatively low.

YELP is a free site (with optional paid upgrades) but I've never joined because I don't like the exposure to rude reviews and no way to reply or give my side of a bogus or negative review.

EBay, for example, allows a person or business to comment to a negative review and discourages negative feedback in general unless all other attempts to resolve a problem have failed.

Yelp and Google do not (at this writing) give that chance to business owners.

7. GOOGLE ACCOUNT

Sign up for a Google account to enjoy better ranking on Google. Always include an address as this increases your placement on Google maps which seem to be of increasing importance.

Some have signed up for multiple accounts for the same business but Google has been connecting phone numbers and other info to figure this out and might de-rank your website if discovered so avoid it or at least be smart about using a different phone number, street address or a website that isn't just a "forwarded website" or other easy way for them to figure out it's the same business.

Sign in to Google. Go to Account, then Google Places, then Add a Business.

Fill out address even if you have a home business. If you don't want customers to know your address or home address, put in a P.O. Box or address of a friend's business (if they don't mind) and best if it's a central or downtown location so your business will be high on the searches for that town. Include a zip code.

Google used to verify many businesses via phone number (so addresses could be omitted or fake), but now it's primarily with postcards sent to that address. You'll receive a verification code to fill in on your Google account (to make it live).

If you put in a fake address, you won't receive the postcard and Google might flag your website, phone number, etc., and it could affect future rankings.

8. GOOGLE IMAGES and PICASA WEB

When you search Google Images, you might be allowing others to use an image (or steal it), so be cautious which images you release.

On the other hand, they can be useful and profitable if it returns customers to your business or service.

Sign into Google.
Go to Accounts, then Products, then Picasa Web.

Take photos of your business, products or the area you serve (ie: a nice photo of your town or a landmark).
Upload into a photo album on Google.
Name the photo album a title similar to keywords but a brief sentence that makes sense on its own.

Release the photo as "Public on the Web" or it will not come up on searches. The default goes to "private" so release it (on upper right of album settings).
If you cannot find this (Google hasn't made this easy to locate), click "Photo Albums" and choose the album (even if it's only one photo it's officially an album) and look for the "Public on the Web" setting. This makes all photos in an album public.

Click on each individual photo to do the settings.
This is what will drive traffic to your image.
Fill in the location. If your business is services not effected by geographic location, you can choose a different location for each photo (L.A., Denver, etc).

TAGS: Choose individual words and name most important words first and if applicable, the towns you serve (including surrounding areas).

I suggest no more than 15 words. You can always choose a different photo to add words not on included on one photo but on another.

DESCRIPTION (under photo itself)

Add a short generic term like
"Affordable Plumbing Services Akron"
Then add your website to include "http://www...."
Now it's a hot link to the website.

I vary my info on photo descriptions to include a hot link only in the description box and in others no link but a keyword type description if the photo has my ph. # or other info that indicates a business name or way to find my business.

In the comment box, you can also add your ph. # or website name, however, it is not as readily seen in the comments section.

You can also add video to your Google Account.

Same rules apply to YouTube title – to be written like keywords but in a brief sentence that makes sense by itself. Don't forget location if applicable.

Different photos can have different keyword type sentences to capture search engines – ie: "Phoenix Wedding Band" on one photo and "Party Planning of Phoenix" on another.

9. QUALITY LINKS

Unlike Link Exchanges (which I never got around to or wanted to do because it could take business away from my site), quality links are websites that have your link but you don't have their link.

This tells Google it's not a link exchange trying to manipulate search results for those businesses engaged in the exchanges but rather a separate business, directory or info site that gives some priority or positive recognition to your business.

IDEAS FOR FREE QUALITY LINKS:

Contact online newspapers and magazines about your business for a story or brief mention. Media likes to print stories or mentions of a new business or an established one that has added a new service, product, etc.

Best to email them and always include your website with the hot link – http://www and hope they print it that way. That is what will be picked up by search engines though sometimes they might write it with the www... only - but it still might be embedded as a hot link even if it doesn't look like it.

The free directories (Denver.com, SanFranciso.com, etc) also become quality links as do the photos/images you upload for Google, etc.

Write an article about your product or service (free tips, etc.) and release it to magazines for your industry, Google Docs, Word Press, etc, and always include the hot link on the article itself. At the bottom of the article is best so it doesn't appear to be an advertisement.

Customers are looking for information and how to decide what to purchase or who to purchase from or hire in a neutral way if possible.

10: VISIT YOUR OWN SITE OFTEN:

When searching for your website, always click through to your site when you see it no matter what page it appears on. Don't visit competitors' websites as it helps keep that business high in ranking.

A competitor's website that is higher placement than your business is worth looking at and studying why.

Instead of clicking on the business from the search results, simply copy and paste or type it into your browser. This avoids giving that website ranking but you can still go to the site and look it over.

Study their content and note the way the content is arranged in one page or in separate boxes.

This is how I taught myself SEO. It took hundreds of hours and now I can pass my knowledge onto you.

Good luck in increasing your search engine ranking and most important, increasing revenue for your business.

Contact me with any specific questions:
BoulderBev@gmail.com

www.ingramcontent.com/pod-product-compliance
Lightning Source LLC
Chambersburg PA
CBHW060937050326
40689CB00013B/3132